The KNOW-NONSENSE Guide to SPACE

Written by Heidi Fiedler

Illustrated by Brendan Kearney

Brimming with creative inspiration, how-to projects, and useful information to enrich your everyday life, Quarto Knows is a favorite destination for those pursuing their interests and passions. Visit our site and dig deeper with our books into your area of interest: Quarto Creates, Quarto Cooks, Quarto Homes, Quarto Lives, Quarto Drives, Quarto Explores, Quarto Gifts, or Quarto Kids.

First Published in 2018 by Walter Foster Jr., an imprint of The Quarto Group.
6 Orchard Road, Suite 100, Lake Forest, CA 92630, USA.
T (949) 380-7510 **F** (949) 380-7575 **www.QuartoKnows.com**

Walter Foster Jr. titles are also available at discount for retail, wholesale, promotional, and bulk purchase. For details, contact the Special Sales Manager by email at specialsales@quarto.com or by mail at The Quarto Group, Attn: Special Sales Manager, 401 Second Avenue North, Suite 310, Minneapolis, MN 55401 USA.

ISBN: 978-1-63322-518-3

Digital edition published in 2018
eISBN: 928-1-63322-519-0

Written by Heidi Fiedler
Illustrated by Brendan Kearney

Printed in China
10 9 8 7 6 5 4 3 2 1

TABLE OF CONTENTS

INTRODUCTION

If **outer space** seems too far to worry about, or you're looking for a funny guide to astronomy, you're in the right place. This book tackles the **key concepts** you need to know about the **solar system, galaxy,** and beyond.

Whether you're curious about **Neptune** or want to know more about **telescopes**, this book will help you navigate the space between the stars.

- Learn about the **planets** in our solar system.
- Dive into a **black hole**.
- Find out where **astronauts** want to go next.

Sound like nonsense? Fear not! By the end of this book, you'll be clear on the difference between a **comet** and an **asteroid,** understand why **Pluto** isn't a planet, and learn what makes the **Milky Way** so milky. Soon you'll go from knowing nothing about space to being a total know-it-all!

THE SOLAR SYSTEM

MERCURY · VENUS · EARTH · MARS

Earth, other planets, moons, asteroids, and more whirl around the sun. This vast place in space is our solar system, and everything caught in the sun's gravity is part of the system. From above, it may look like an oversized game of marbles. But zoom in, and you'll find dazzling details, intriguing mysteries, and interstellar nonsense of the highest order.

*Planets not to scale

SATURN

URANUS

NEPTUNE

PLUTO
(DWARF PLANET)

JUPITER

THE SUN

The sun is the star that everything
in the solar system revolves around.

There are over 100 billion stars in the Milky Way galaxy, but our planet revolves around just one: **the sun**. From Earth's point of view, the sun is the most important star in the sky. It makes up 99 percent of the solar system's mass, gives off light and heat, drives the weather on Earth, and supports life—including us! Like other stars, the sun is a gigantic, hot ball of glowing gas. About one million Earths could fit inside the sun. Temperatures at the core reach 27 million degrees Fahrenheit (15 million degrees Celsius), and the outer layer, known as the corona, reaches temperatures of 3.5 million degrees Fahrenheit (2 million degrees Celsius). The sun's gravity affects everything in the solar system, from the largest planets to the smallest asteroid. It's no exaggeration to say everything revolves around the sun.

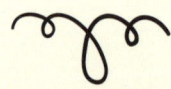

MERCURY

Mercury is the closest planet to the sun.

———•———

Hee! Hoo! Hot! If you've ever tiptoed across scorching hot sand at the beach, you have some idea of what it might be like to land on **Mercury**. A small, dense, and intensely hot planet, Mercury is a difficult place to study since it orbits so close to the sun. So much of this airless place remains a mystery. We do know the surface is covered in craters and deep wrinkles. Below the surface there's a large, metallic core. And because of the way the planet spins around the sun, you might see a double sunrise if you stood on the surface. The sweltering sun first appears in the sky, moves back toward the horizon, and then starts rising again. That might leave you feverish!

DIAMETER	AVERAGE DISTANCE FROM THE SUN	TIME TO ORBIT SUN (A YEAR)	TIME TO SPIN ON AXIS (A DAY)
3,031 MILES (4,878 KM)	36,000,000 MILES (57,900,000 KM)	88 DAYS	59 DAYS

VENUS

Venus is the planet closest to Earth.

When you're a heavenly body named after the ancient Roman goddess of love and beauty, you might expect aliens to swoon. But any swooning that happens on **Venus** is more likely caused by how intensely hot the planet is. The thick atmosphere traps heat, so temperatures can reach over 800 degrees Fahrenheit (427 degrees Celsius) on the second planet from the sun. The atmosphere is also poisonous, and acid rains down from a thick layer of clouds. And at the very top of Venus's mountains, there is a layer of snow. But not as we know it! Snow on Venus is made from frozen metal.

DIAMETER	AVERAGE DISTANCE FROM THE SUN	TIME TO ORBIT SUN (A YEAR)	TIME TO SPIN ON AXIS (A DAY)
7,521 MILES (12,104 KM)	67,000,000 MILES (108,160,000 KM)	224 DAYS	243 DAYS

EARTH

Earth is the planet we live on.

Earth is like the baby bear's porridge from "Goldilocks and the Three Bears." Not too hot and not too cold, the third planet from the sun is just right for human life. It's the only planet in our solar system that has liquid water on the surface. In fact, it's the only planet in the whole universe that has life (that we know of)! At over 4 billion years old, Earth has existed much longer than humans, animals, plants, and even simple cells. And while it's not alive, it is still changing. Earth's core, mantle, and crust cause everything from mountains to fault lines to move. But for now, and hopefully the next billion years, Earthlings are lucky to call this planet home sweet home.

DIAMETER	AVERAGE DISTANCE FROM THE SUN	TIME TO ORBIT SUN (A YEAR)	TIME TO SPIN ON AXIS (A DAY)
7,926 MILES (12,756 KM)	92,960,000 MILES (149,600,000 KM)	365.25 DAYS	23 HOURS, 56 MINS

THE MOON

The moon is a large rock that circles Earth.

The moon orbits Earth night and day. Astronomers think it formed when Earth was hit by a planet from outer space, causing a chunk of rock to break off. Today, the moon is less than half the size of Earth and has similar layers: a core, mantle, and crust. The surface is covered in craters. Earthlings landed on the moon in 1969. But the moon is more than a place for astronauts to bounce in low gravity. It influences Earth even from afar, affecting the oceans' tides and making our climate human-friendly. That's what friends are for, right?

DIAMETER	AVERAGE DISTANCE FROM EARTH	TIME TO ORBIT EARTH (A YEAR)
2,160 MILES (3,475 KM)	238,857 MILES (384,400 KM)	27 DAYS

MARS

Mars is a small, red planet.

Besides our beloved Earth, **Mars** is the planet that we know the most about. Small, rocky, and cold, the fourth planet appears as a bright red light in the sky. The surface is coated in a fine red dust that's rich in rusted iron. The weather is wild with huge tornadoes and dust avalanches. The surface is home to the biggest volcanoes in the solar system. Long ago the planet was wet, but all that remains now is ice. Most exciting of all? It's possible life formed there before it did on Earth. And while there's no sign of life on Mars today, Earthlings might one day move there and become Martians!

DIAMETER	AVERAGE DISTANCE FROM THE SUN	TIME TO ORBIT SUN (A YEAR)	TIME TO SPIN ON AXIS (A DAY)
4,222 MILES (6,794 KM)	141,700,000 MILES (227,936,640 KM)	687 DAYS	24 HOURS, 37 MINS

JUPITER

Jupiter is the largest planet in the solar system.

Jupiter is so gigantic that all the other planets in the solar system could fit inside it. It's warm, gassy, and covered in thick clouds that flow in opposite directions. The Great Red Spot is a huge hurricane that's been roaring for over 300 years and is larger than our entire planet. Under the clouds, there's no hard surface, just a thick layer of gases that turn into liquids the deeper you go. It might have a rocky, metal core, but scientists aren't sure. Want to know some nonsense? While the fifth planet from the sun is enormous and hugely fascinating, its days are surprisingly short. It rotates faster than any other planet in the solar system, making a day there just under 10 hours long.

DIAMETER	AVERAGE DISTANCE FROM THE SUN	TIME TO ORBIT SUN (A YEAR)	TIME TO SPIN ON AXIS (A DAY)
88,846 MILES (142,984 KM)	483,500,000 MILES (778,369,000 KM)	11.86 YEARS	9 HOURS, 55 MINS

SATURN

Saturn is a gas planet surrounded by icy rings.

Saturn is the beauty queen of the solar system. A single glance at its rings has inspired many to become astronomers. Like Jupiter, Saturn is a giant gas planet covered in a thick layer of clouds. At its north pole, a six-sided vortex of storms blows over 300 miles (483 km) per hour. And there's likely a rocky core below. At least 60 moons orbit the sixth planet from the sun. With temperatures below -250 degrees Fahrenheit (-157 degrees Celsius), the planet is extremely cold. Even the gorgeous rings are made of billions of small chunks of ice. So perhaps this beauty should be known as the ice queen instead!

DIAMETER	AVERAGE DISTANCE FROM THE SUN	TIME TO ORBIT SUN (A YEAR)	TIME TO SPIN ON AXIS (A DAY)
74,900 MILES (120,536 KM)	888,750,000 MILES (1,427,034,000 KM)	29 YEARS	10 HOURS, 39 MINS

URANUS

Uranus is a distant gas planet that rotates on its side.

Whether you pronounce it *you-run-us*, *YOU-run-us*, *you-RAY-nus*, or *OOO-ran-ose*, **Uranus** is the solar system's goofiest planet. It spins far out in the solar system, appearing as a faint blue light in telescopes. It's almost 15 times bigger than Earth, but it's not very dense. Astronomers believe there's a small rocky core surrounded by a thick icy mantle, which is covered by a thick atmosphere. Diamond hail may blow inside the clouds that smell like rotten eggs, and an ocean of liquid diamonds is thought to lie below. But the goofiest trait is Uranus's tilt. Most planets spin counterclockwise. But Uranus is tipped on its side, so it rotates perpendicular to the sun. That makes the weather there super strange, and gives the seventh planet its reputation as being more than a little weird.

DIAMETER	AVERAGE DISTANCE FROM THE SUN	TIME TO ORBIT SUN (A YEAR)	TIME TO SPIN ON AXIS (A DAY)
31,763 MILES (51,118 KM)	1,783,744,300 MILES (2,870,658,186 KM)	84 YEARS	17 HOURS, 14 MINS

NEPTUNE

Neptune is the most distant planet in the solar system.

Astronomers scored a victory when **Neptune** became the first planet to be predicted before being seen in the sky. Astronomers noticed that Uranus was being pulled out of orbit, and after some math calculations, they predicted another planet was the culprit. Observations have shown it's similar to Uranus, but denser and deeper blue. Neptune's orbit around the sun is almost perfectly circular, so its distance from the sun doesn't vary much as it travels around the sun. The orbit causes seasons that produce warmer spots on the planet. The contrast between the planet's temperature and the deep cold space that surrounds it causes wild winds, an effect that any Earthlings—or other alien visitors who might travel there—are sure to notice.

DIAMETER	AVERAGE DISTANCE FROM THE SUN	TIME TO ORBIT SUN (A YEAR)	TIME TO SPIN ON AXIS (A DAY)
30,779 MILES (49,532 KM)	2,797,770,000 MILES (4,496,976,000 KM)	164.8 YEARS	16 HOURS, 7 MINS

PLUTO

Pluto is a dwarf planet on the outer edge of the solar system.

Once considered a planet, **Pluto** was downgraded to dwarf status in 2006 when astronomers found icy worlds similar in size to Pluto drifting beyond Neptune. Today Pluto is considered part of the Kuiper belt, an area made up of thousands of pieces of floating ice and rock. The wannabe planet is lethally cold and covered in mountains that tower above an icy landscape. Scientists are always responding to new data, and as they learn more about planets, the definition might change to once again include Pluto. But that would also add more than one hundred other "planets" to the solar system!

DIAMETER	AVERAGE DISTANCE FROM THE SUN	TIME TO ORBIT SUN (A YEAR)	TIME TO SPIN ON AXIS (A DAY)
1,473 MILES (2,370 KM)	3,670,050,000 MILES (5,906,380,000 KM)	248 YEARS	6 DAYS, 9 HOURS

ASTEROID BELT

The asteroid belt is a large group of rocks that orbit the sun between Mars and Jupiter.

Despite its name, the **asteroid belt** isn't something you can buckle. It's actually an area between Mars and Jupiter that contains lots of asteroids. The solar system is home to billions of these chunky pieces of rock and metal. They come in all different shapes and sizes—one even looks like a dog bone! Surprisingly, the asteroid belt is actually mostly empty space. If you stood on an asteroid, most of the other asteroids would be too far away to be seen with your eyes. But use a telescope, and you'll find a different view. Astronomers spend lots of time scoping out asteroids and calculating if any will collide with Earth. So it's best they keep those eyes on the sky!

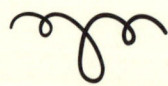

COMETS

Comets are pieces of ice and dust that orbit the sun.

Sky gazers once imagined **comets** could reveal the future.
Now we understand they're similar to asteroids, just a little more icy.
Comets have a solid body that's made up of ice and dust particles.
That's why astronomers sometimes call comets dirty snowballs.
When comets pass close to the sun, the outer layer of ice quickly turns
to gas, known as the coma, and the effect can be extraordinarily bright.
Comets also have two kinds of tails. If you see a blue light trailing the
comet, that's the ion tail, which is created when the solar wind blows the
coma gas away from the sun. A white or yellow tail forms when sunlight
pushes the dust from the comet into a long curving tail. It's a beautiful
way to say "see ya soon!" to the sun.

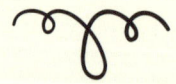

THE OORT CLOUD

The Oort cloud is made up of trillions of pieces of ice that surround the solar system far past Neptune.

Scientists are foggy on how far the sun's influence reaches, so they don't know exactly how big our solar system is. But they think it's surrounded by an enormous, icy bubble. The mysterious **Oort cloud** is home to trillions of pieces of ice. The region is too far for astronomers to keep an eye on it with telescopes. In fact, the cloud hasn't even officially been discovered yet. But scientists are confident it's there. It's thought that many of the comets that sail through our solar system come from the Oort cloud, and more pieces of ice might become comets if something collides at just the right angle to send them into the inner solar system. It can all feel too distant too worry about, but if a large comet is headed straight for Earth, we won't want to miss it!

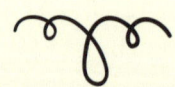

GALAXIES

Galaxies are groups of gas, space dust, and hundreds of billions of stars. Galaxies come in four main shapes and are huge—as big as hundreds of thousands of light-years across.

One light-year equals about 5.88 trillion miles (9.45 trillion km)!

Irregular galaxies don't have a clear shape and include a mishmash of bright areas and some dark areas.

Spiral galaxies are circular, symmetrical, and include older stars in the center and younger stars in the outer arms.

Scientists estimate that there are more than 1,000,000,000,000 (that's a hundred billion!) galaxies in the universe. Now that's a galactic number of galaxies!

Elliptical galaxies are longer, less defined, and mostly made of older stars. They have much less gas and dust in them.

Lenticular galaxies are thin with a bright center and a faint outer layer.

THE MILKY WAY

The Milky Way is home to our solar system and billions of other planets and stars.

Trying to understand where we are in **the Milky Way** is a bit like mapping the inside of a hurricane while the wind is blowing all around you. It's tricky to get the right perspective. From above, the Milky Way looks like a flat disk that measures 100,000 light-years wide. There's a bulge in the middle, two huge, sweeping arms, and two shorter, spiral arms. The larger spiral arms contain the biggest, brightest stars. This is also where most stars are born. At the edge, a halo of old stars surrounds the galaxy, while a bar of billions of old red stars lies near the middle. Giving new meaning to the word "twister," it all revolves around a monster black hole that's four million times more massive than the sun.

GALAXY TYPE	DIAMETER
SPIRAL	100,000 LIGHT-YEARS

THE SUN

ANDROMEDA GALAXY

The Andromeda Galaxy is the closest large galaxy to the Milky Way.

On a clear, moonless night, the **Andromeda Galaxy** looks like a milky blur to the naked eye. It's 2.5 million light-years from Earth and similar to the Milky Way, but way bigger and with more stars. Telescopes reveal it's moving toward us at 100 kilometers per second. It will most likely collide with the Milky Way in several billion years (yikes!), merging to form a jumbo galaxy called Milkomeda (groan). At least there's time for scientists to come up with a better name for the new galaxy.

GALAXY TYPE	DIAMETER
SPIRAL	220,000 LIGHT-YEARS

THE MILKY WAY

NEBULA

A nebula is a large cloud of gas and dust where stars are born.

Goo-goo, ga-ga! Known as the nurseries of the universe, **nebulae** are the glowing places in space where stars are born. Some are small and dense. Others are mostly empty clouds that spread several light-years wide. When stars die, they release clouds of gas that become nebulae. Gravity causes the cloud to contract. The nebula grows denser and hotter until finally it becomes so hot that the hydrogen inside bursts into flame. And a new star is born. The colors of the glowing light reveal the elements inside. Now who's a cute little starling?

STAR

A star is a massive body of gas that creates its own energy and light through nuclear fusion.

Twinkle, twinkle, little star, how I wonder what you are. For thousands of years, people have gazed at the night sky, inventing constellations and telling stories. But if you look closer, these points of light are actually huge, fiery balls of gas. Hot, dense, and wildly active, **stars** create energy and light through a process called *nuclear fusion*. Nuclear fusion happens when hydrogen and helium atoms join together in the core. As stars age, they change in size, color, and temperature. Astronomers classify stars into seven different types. Hotter stars radiate brighter blue light, and cooler ones radiate red. Our sun is classified as a G star, based off its yellow color and temperature.

CLASS	O	B	A	F	G	K	M
TEMPERATURE (KELVIN*)	33,000 OR MORE	10,500– 30,000	7,500– 10,000	6,000– 7,200	5,500– 6,000	4,000– 5,250	2,600– 3,850

*0 DEGREES CELSIUS = 32 DEGREES FAHRENHEIT = 273 KELVIN

LIFE CYCLE OF A STAR

Stars change and go through a series of stages over billions of years.

Stars aren't alive, but astronomers talk about them as if they are. Stars are formed when gravity pulls dust and gas together. Eventually gravity is so strong that nuclear fusion occurs, and a star is born. During its main sequence stage, a star will produce energy for 10 billion years. (Our sun is in this stage.) When it runs out of fuel, it will expand and cool into a red giant. Then the outer layers will blow off, and it will become a white dwarf star. Finally it will turn into a black dwarf, which is the cool, dark thing that remains when nothing else is left.

Larger stars can collapse and explode into stunningly bright supernovas. Then they transform into massive black holes or extremely dense neutron stars. No matter what size they started, stars will release most of their gas and dust back into the galaxy, allowing new stars to be born. That's why poets know it's not nonsense to talk about us and everything else in the universe being made of stardust!

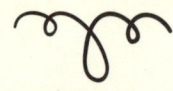

MAIN SEQUENCE STAR

RED GIANT

WHITE DWARF

BLACK DWARF

SUPERNOVA

NEBULA

NEUTRON STAR

BLACK HOLE

BLACK HOLE

A black hole is a place in space
where gravity is so intense that nothing,
not even light, can escape.

Black holes form when massive stars use all their fuel and collapse. The intense gravity happens when matter is pulled into the hole and compressed into a mind-bogglingly small space. It's infinitely dense, which is an idea that's infinitely hard to understand. The area of space that surrounds the black hole is called *the event horizon,* because events that happen beyond it can't be known. Black holes are intensely powerful, but you need to be close to feel their effect. Scientists think most galaxies rotate around supermassive black holes. A black hole that's more than 4 million times more massive than the sun lies at the center of our galaxy. Hole-y wow!

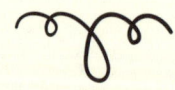

EXPLORING SPACE

In 1961, the first human was launched into space. Since then, we've landed on the moon, explored Mars, and sent probes out past the solar system. Today *Voyager 1* is floating 12 billion miles (19 billion km) away from the Earth, sending back data from interstellar space. Whatever alien nonsense it will find next is a question scientists can't wait to know the answer to!

TELESCOPE

A telescope is an instrument used to view distant objects in more detail by focusing light with mirrors or lenses.

When it comes to studying outer space, squinting will only get you so far. **Telescopes** reveal details that are invisible to the naked eye, including Saturn's rings, craters on the moon, and distant galaxies. Telescopes use a glass lens or a mirror to hold light, the same way a bucket holds water. The bigger the bucket, the more water it can hold. And the bigger the telescope, the more light it can gather. Long telescopes funnel and focus light. As they get longer and wider, they can show us fainter and fainter objects. Launching telescopes into space lets us look beyond our atmosphere, which blurs and distorts objects in the sky. So squint no more, scientists!

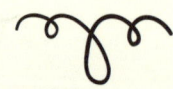

SATELLITES

Satellites are devices designed to orbit Earth, moon, or other planets.

Telescopes aren't the only eyes we have in our skies. *Sputnik* was the first satellite to orbit the Earth. Robots, the space station, and space shuttles are all **satellites** too. They help scientists do research. People also rely on satellites to make cell phones work, forecast the weather, and find places with GPS technology. Spies use them to track enemies.

We keep putting more and more satellites into space, so it's starting to feel like a high-speed garbage dump, with satellites discarded like trash. The good news is scientists are busy developing self-destructing satellites that will crash and burn when we no longer need them instead of floating around as space waste. It's a no-nonsense approach that can help us explore space for years to come!

ASTRONAUT

An astronaut is someone who travels in a spacecraft.

Imagine being the first person to walk on Mars or to fly light-years across the galaxy to a planet that has yet to be discovered. **Astronauts** may have the coolest job in the entire universe. They're explorers, scientists, and leaders all rolled into one. The training is intense—you'll need to study math, science, and engineering and fly for at least 1,000 hours—and every mission requires bravery. But when launch day arrives, it's worth it! The possibilities are truly out of this world!

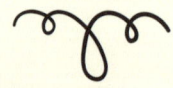

ROBOT

A robot is a machine that looks or acts like a human being, performing tasks that humans cannot do or choose not to do.

Humans haven't traveled beyond the moon, but **robots** have explored Mars, Venus, comets, asteroids, and other areas of space that may be too dangerous for humans. The robots are tested here on Earth in places that are similar to Mars or the moon, like the arid deserts of Arizona or frozen tundra of Iceland. The missions are suspenseful because no one knows how they will perform millions of miles away. But the results have been spectacular. Now scientists are designing submarines to drift through the oceans of Europa (one of Jupiter's moons), spacecraft to orbit comets, and more. One of the most well known robots, the Mars Curiosity Rover, has special tools for taking samples, analyzing the planet, and looking for signs of life. It can even sing "Happy Birthday!"

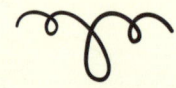

INTERNATIONAL SPACE STATION

The International Space Station (ISS) is a large spacecraft that orbits around the Earth and houses astronauts and other scientists.

The **International Space Station** is an enormous laboratory built by scientists and engineers from countries around the world. The first piece was sent up in 1998. It took two years for the station to be ready for people to live there, and another eleven years for the station to be finished. Now it's nearly the size of a football field, with two bathrooms, a gym, and room for six people. NASA (the National Aeronautics and Space Administration) and other space agencies use the station to study what it's like to live and work in space, as well as do research that can't be done on Earth. It's an important step toward taking longer journeys and exploring deep space. So what do ISS astronauts call our home planet when they're orbiting above us? Spaceship Earth, of course!

A NOTE TO KNOW-IT-ALLS

Stargazing might feel a little different now that you know the difference between a **comet** and an **asteroid,** what makes a **planet** a planet, and why what happens in a **black hole** stays in a black hole. But it would be a mistake to think you—or anyone else—knows everything there is to know about space. That's part of what makes outer space so **amazing.** It's bigger, stranger, and wilder than we can imagine. And thinking we might ever know it all is utter nonsense!